rife

rife

poems

Stefanie Marlis

Sarabande Books

LOUISVILLE, KENTUCKY

Managing Editor
Sarabande Books, Inc.
2234 Dundee Road, Suite 200
Louisville, KY 40205

LIBRARY OF CONGRESS CATALOGING-IN-PUBLICATION DATA

Marlis, Stefanie,
    Rife : poems / by Stefanie Marlis.
        p. cm.
    ISBN 1-889330-11-6 (cloth : alk. paper). — ISBN 1-889330-12-4
    (pbk. : alk. paper)
    I. Title.
    PS3563.A6735R54 1998
    811'.54—dc21   97-10568 CIP

Cover: Kamisakka Sekka, Japanese, 1866–1942. *Deer Amid the Pines* from *The World of Things*, 1910–1911. Three-volume wood blocks printed in color with gold and silver. © The Cleveland Museum of Art, 1997, Norman O. Stone and Ella A. Stone Memorial Fund, 1988.23–.24–.25.

Lines from "Deer" are reprinted from *Flamingo Watching* © 1994 by Kay Ryan, by permission of Copper Beech Press.

Cover typography by Sharrie Brooks.

Manufactured in the United States of America.
This book is printed on acid-free paper.

Sarabande Books is a nonprofit literary organization.

For Robert Oliver

rife. I say rife, with deer.
For if one leaf against the littered floor
be cleft with the true arc,
all this lost ground, and more,
becomes a park.

Kay Ryan

Acknowledgments

American Poetry Review: "Dog"

Arshile: "e-mail," "spring   coming on"

Denver Quarterly: "Carnival"

Five Fingers Review: "Change," "Chignon"

The Gettysburg Review: "Butter," "Proteus & Sunflowers," "Hollywood"

Manoa: "Bells," "Days," "Scorpion" (Previously titled "Devolution")

The Massachusetts Review: "Sheet of Glass," "Instead"

New Letters: "Paths"

Ploughshares: "Meditation"

Poetry: "Saturn," "Stardust"

Poetry Flash: "Pigeons"

Volt: "surprise   coming on"

Zyzzyva: "echo," "ersatz," "flit," "leitmotif," "proffer," "quash," "rife,"
        "rule," "shibboleth"

A number of these poems were published in a chapbook, *Sheet of Glass*, Floating Island Press, 1994.

My gratitude to the National Endowment for the Arts for its assistance during the writing of this manuscript.

Table of Contents

Dog

Last night, I was given a choice of waking in a world
where everyone was kind and good but still mortal
or in another where we were as we are
but lived forever.
Then the dream fell apart like certain blossoms do
as soon as they are picked, and I was too sick all day
to think about anything but things:
a new coat, black-and-white china from Arizona.
And what about this skinny, dappled dog—
is my affection for him just part of exhaustion.
What if the afterlife were shaped like a dog. What if,
lying between this dingo puppy and my old retriever,
I feel my affections balancing without subtraction.
Isn't there an everlastingness in that.
What if the next life shines like the sun—a noon-life,
the heart so high and big it's shadowless.
I'm not afraid of sweetness—what if what follows
is shaped like a pear.
Or sharpened to a triangle, the mind bobbing in one corner,
the soul pausing in another,
and God in the third—sewing curtains, crating
lettuce, fitting pipe, shoveling snow,
adding columns, hunting deer, driving carpool,
placing offtrack bets, feeding sparrows—
as many as names in a phone book—flying down
from the wires?

Sheet of Glass

You run into them,
shopping, the ones who were almost too good to you—
faces tanned, hands stronger than you remember. And even though
you may have the same bag of apples, carrots, in your cart,
in "his" they look so much better.

And you think back to why, in the end, you decided
no. You were taken with his stories,
with the way he listened to yours, but finally,
in his office or your kitchen, you made the admission
and turned away.

Like the fish—
for some reason the lesson has stayed with me.
The fish and the sheet of glass. How,
my science teacher explained, they would continue
to turn back at the center of the tank,
even after the glass was gone, and the whole length lay open.

heed—to pay careful attention to, traceable to the German *hüten*, to guard, akin to hood—which is what her caring had become, something she pulled up around her, protecting her, narrowing her vision as well. Tonight, she's rented a movie, Bogart, her ex's look-alike, and notices the roses, even more present in the dim light, have filled the room with their scent; she breathes: if only his were not his.

Carnival

An enormous man takes tickets for a ride on which the smallest children,
stationed in hot rods and rockets, merry-go-round.

How he seems to love his work. Uncommonly ugly, so obese his body
is running out of room to store the fat—

so it collects everywhere: under his ears and in big pockets
around his genitals. His voice is squeaky but sweet

and patient with these tiny prizes, teasing gently,
preparing them for the ride.

And when it is over, he unbuckles his treasures, being always careful
not to touch them.

Instead

Who hasn't mistaken the tip of a black shoe
for a mouse? A tissue for a rain-soaked rose—a rose
for a toad? And who hasn't gestured to a stranger
as if to an old friend?
How easy, then, for the world itself to be mistaken.
To grow a tumor instead of a walnut. To take the flesh
of a good man for sugar, for sand, and blow it away.
A small boy stands in the yard on the most beautiful day
of the year, throwing sand up in the air, yelling
I want something to rain down, and his mother saying,
to the son of the good man, *We'll turn on the hose.*

Saturn

I am learning not to measure perfection
like sugar.
Mike's son, at twelve years, one hundred
pounds,
can't tell time, can't add a quarter apple
to a half,
or clear the dishes without forgetting
midway.
But he is perfecting one art. Call it patience
or limits.
Orbits—the lark no less for the hawk gliding
higher.
For Christmas, he's been given a telescope;
by nightfall
it is set beneath the freshly inked
dome.
Out there the showiest star's
a planet.
He loves the buoyant, frictionless
plate
his father has in focus. Miscounts moons.
Pleasure aura. Call it perfect.

Dangerous Archipelagoes

A man takes a break from his paperwork and stands thousands of miles away—on the deck of a boat in the South Pacific—years ago. He hears the water lapping on the hull and the voices below. The light pours down from the stars, from holes punched in the top of a shoe box. Everything, they say, has its time and its place. He's doing his taxes; Jupiter is about to be struck by a comet; and he remembers a man old enough to be his father walking around on deck with one shoe.

The World

It's the friend pulling you aside:
You know the tendency you have to always—
It's a risky thing for any friend to do,
but at that moment
the red bowl in your kitchen takes you as far
as the planet Mars.

The voice of the wide sea or a thunderstorm—
a threaded needle pulling you
to the other side of the cloth, trying with every shape,
with every sound to tell you about another way.

Trying anything—a mouth slowly turning
to a smile, a team of horses with tassels, voices escaping
through an open window, a man on a cross, unidentified
flying objects—anything to get you there.

Candies

Years ago her boss would find her, a young girl below a moon-sized kitchen clock, sliding store-made chocolates into their paper nests, never tasting the chocolate, always washing it from her fingers. There she'd be listening to the day dawn on the radio, waiting for those faces she'd come to love to appear on the other side of the high white counter—mystery writer, mechanic, priest. She never married. Cared for her mother until the end. Good Friday—a customer pauses in the entrance on Fourth Street—and she smiles from behind the gold foil rabbits, as if it is her very first day, weighs out the candies trusting love as measurable and sweet.

proffer—to put before a person for acceptance, from the Old French *por*,

pro + *offrir*, to offer—so she dressed, carefully, with allure: flippy skirt,

shirt the shade of blue grass, following through on a gathering impulse.

At a coffeehouse, she watches a couple against a green wall kiss, and she

barters with God, like a child offering a little toe in exchange, for what

she thinks they have.

Orbits

A boy watching TV dangles his feet over the armrest
so his father will tickle them—an ongoing game.

Not far away, up on the rain-soaked hill
where vultures have been circling like black notes,

police discover a missing person. Father and son laugh:
how silly the show is—*there's no such thing.*

The boy pulls a puppet from his collection of toys,
and the blond dog curled up on the bed shakes her head.

When he walks through the gate of his other house,
his mother's, he is a boy who believes in ghosts.

technique—the procedure by which a task is accomplished, from the Greek *tekhnikos*, of art—repeatedly the artful way he undertakes to spoil the charge between them: by telling her of a friend's incontinent mother soiling the couch or the grunge of his son's underwear, his own bouts of indigestion; inasmuch as he remains her flower, the fetid images growing beautifully fecund around any mention of his body, his method fails.

Buttons

Letterpress, he says, *is a peripheral art, like magic.* Like a kid making angels on a clean page of snow. He rises early and launches M's queenly as cruise ships, seats O's you want to use as buttons. He has a soft spot for Z's. He does not work to please a world happy with ink-jet, instant, offset, but for the printed word itself. He sets a broadside in a hefty serif, a birth announcement in a tall Futura. As easily as the rest of us tell three o'clock from six, he recognizes Albertus, Garamond, Bembo, Bell. And each character strikes the page like a bell, and dwells there—an inked figure buried, burrowing in the white earth. *Here, give me your finger,* he says, and runs it along a line, *feel the halo around each letter.*

for Peter Koch

leitmotif—a recurring theme, from the Old High German *leitmotiv*, lead + motion—on the way, he gleefully told another story about an accident involving pea gravel. This time, a truckload rained down on a cherried-out blue Falcon. Yet the movie was too much for him; he couldn't bear a broken heart, his or anyone else's, which led to an obsession with video games and science fiction.

e - m a i l

Someone left the light on, she wrote of the evolution of the rose.
A rose, not gloves, not butter, but the utterly
ornamental. That's the joy of mail coming forth
across the ocean, sweeping plains, snowy mountains.
Writes about the waiters' race through the city,
balancing glasses on trays, about the Concourse of Roses!
Tonight, in the last light, leaning the broom
against the wall, I thought of the wavelengths
set into motion—snowballs gathering roses—lovely verbs
streaming outward, ho, nouns. The spark, arc between
two working hearts settling for words.

for Cole Swensen

Meditation

The world sneaks back. Like the small dog that lives up the street,
small enough he needn't wait for her to open the gate.

Alone, she goes farther inside where the shore's swept
so clean it becomes meaningless.

And that's the beauty of it, looking down the beach
it's empty, a long well of sunlight and heat,

until she hears the terrier's unclipped nails
and the rain and wind pick up—tiny bits of sea glass.

No, she says, her own dog hearing too, *he stinks.*
All right, she says, getting up to let the other dog in.

rife—in widespread existence or use, from the Old Icelandic *rifr*, abundant—"they're on fire," she thinks, of the slim trailside trees burning with green flames. A lush, new season! And she's practiced the theory all week, "abundance thinking." It's true; there's so much of so much: moss, stars, dumpster agleam with the worst of what an old man couldn't take with him.

Traps

There's a hole in the ceiling covered with brown paper,
and three clocks and three mousetraps in various locations.

One tiny alien, lured by kibble, suffering just one injured paw,
now lies cold, nestled in a makeshift mouse-house.

As the death is discussed, a button mysteriously appears
on the table, a pearly disc not missing from anything

anyone's wearing. *Oh, well;* someone stands up
and puts on some water. Then suddenly

(it's been raining hard all morning), great jarfuls
of buttons pour down from the gutters.

rule—an authoritative prescription for conduct, from the Latin *regula*, rod—as simple as: whatever you wish that others would do onto you, do onto them. He entered from behind, twice, a little difficult at first: lots of lubricant and patience. The next morning, as she went into the kitchen thinking pancakes, he was already measuring: flour, milk, eggs, salt.

M y t h

The air inside the range: cold, leaden; she fires
       at the paper target, dark holes clustering—
which is the sport, thrill
of lining up eye, sight, bull's-eye—
       the metaphysics of bullet, Eros, anger—
         anything requiring a mark.

The man she's come with loves
       shooting;
she watches as he loads and unloads his gun—
just as that morning he folded the sheets
       matching corner to corner, exactly.

for Bruce Brodie

chignon—a bun worn above the neck, from the Old French *chaignon*, chain—likewise the red bud tree stands in its rosy chains in the civil twilight. Even if there were a way to untie the future as a woman unties her hair, one might not. She swore she'd wait but could not keep herself: three-beat knock; and she let him go there, there, to where untolled atoms jump ship per second, as if she had known he wanted a child.

Paths

Two days later their dictionaries remain open to the same page in the F's. A man had called a woman he used to love, asking about the Fates—who spun? who measured? who snipped?—imagining the three clothed in mossy robes, stooped and deadpan. To the west, beyond the town, where evening already is, one of the gray lanky clouds sports a goatee. *The devil,* the woman mouths, though every other man on the street, it seems, has grown one. A thought crawls up to her: *I am just like my mother.* A few blocks away, a hundred-year-old oak lies across a stream; the storm that felled a couple thousand trees has changed the light in the creekside house forever, yet just around the corner—persimmons—ten fire-orange globes stud a petite tree. Not knowing, it makes sense to assume that whatever is belongs.

Proteus & Sunflowers

Now that you've been reminded of how easily
this sand can be swept away,

you try to set your plate down with more care,
to pick the apricots or watch them fall,

and Dorianne has a cigarette, then smokes another
for Robert, just out of surgery.

Outside, a succession of summer days, little blue fish
chased by bigger and bigger fish. And the girl

in the dream arranges proteus and huge sunflowers
that sit by your friend's bedside in a cobalt vase.

You hear from another Robert, from twenty years ago
in San Francisco, what now seems another life,

and coincidence spawns coincidence,
until the world means what it's meant to mean;

the blue fish eaten, the cut-flowers nevertheless
still drinking.

ilk—type or kind, from the Old English *ilca*, same—one calls the other,

knowing the papers on her table and tall bamboo are riffled by the same

westerly wind that has just swept through her friend's, disturbing the

marbled coy in the oval pond. And when she listens to her friend's fears,

her own are quickly stirred, like the fish flying through the tangle of lilies.

Tree Frogs

Hopper, Jumper, and the biggest—Leaper.
No, he says,
I just want to call them My Three Frogs.
He understands about fate already.
God sits at a kitchen table, a twin to your own,
and dials your number. The trick is to know
how to take cues from the conversation—
it's a matter of letting some things go
while nudging others toward what you want.
The last creature the boy caught, a field mouse
he named Mikie, escaped while we went for burritos.

Scorpion

The night I return from Los Angeles
I visit Mars—
there, once again, are Hollywood's
blighted mini-malls
and the clownish, mop-topped palms
of riot city.
Later, when the tremor
of a Martian earthquake
wakes me,
I join Giordano's scorpion
in the midnight kitchen—
with a luckless moth bucking
like a lassoed pony
inside the round aquarium.
After cartoons the next morning,
we lift off the copper screen top
and remove, with six-inch tweezers,
frayed wings and the sucked-out thorax
thrown down,
spiraling
like a glove.

Skunks

The motion-sensitive light behind the bamboo shade
is on, tripped by the coterie of skunks
my neighbor tries to drive away by playing a radio
and lighting up his basement like a space station.
They get into places where their bodies cannot go but do.
By morning their stink will have faded with the moon,
and the skunks will become again a joke shared across a fence.
How easily it converts: a dark thought, like a stain,
into white cloth; starlight into the little holes of a colander
through which a lifetime streams.

Pigeons

On Earth he sold tires in a small town that smelled of wet dogs. Which is where he started practicing. He's not sure how he ended up in tires. He was convinced that if he spent all his evenings, an hour in the morning before work, and all day Sunday—he could do it. He began with a cup of coffee. Mastering coffee, he moved on to clouds, pushing them around the sky, first the ones that looked like swans, then the mobile homes and tankers. Soon it was tires—out back, after everyone was gone—several got as high as the roof, startling the pigeons. He watched them fly from their roost and swoop down on the House of Donuts two towns away. Now, he could start—he could move mountains, he could bring peace to Earth.

shibboleth—a catchword, from the Hebrew *sibbolet,* a torrent of water—

at the fords of the Jordan one tribe tried to slip across disguised as another

and was caught as they could not say *sh.* "Any redneck missing teeth and

fingers can weld," he declares. Having grown up along the Mississippi and

eager to distinguish himself from those working there on the barges.

Lizard

He tried to imagine another life and could not. He was a lizard blissfully lounging on a lavender rock. He tried to imagine another sun and could not. He came back as a man who owned a small company that installed window shades. His wife and two sons worked with him. He was an energetic man (once he got going), and in many ways the hard work suited him. But this time of year was the busiest, and he longed for big starry nights in the high desert, copper canyons, and leisurely mornings in the sun. This year, he promised himself, he would enjoy the little things: the bells, the fresh scent of evergreen, reindeer on the roofs. *This is all there is*, he said to himself (having read many philosophical books).

* *The first and third lines echo lines from Czeslaw Milosz's poem "From the Rising Sun."*

Flesh

Manta rays, Hawaii, soft circling records in the floodlights,
such creatureliness against the black lava rocks, the flesh of figs, pigs,
earthworms—that that leaves us first, death stripping us to the bone.

First day of daylight-saving—glorious, windless blue—a shirtless man
on a ten-speed pulls up to a woman in a red dress at a red light;
green, but they linger, his torso, her bare arm in the potable sun.

There was nothing to say in the dying man's room;
she looked at a picture on his wall: him holding up his naked son
in a swimming pool and thought how beautiful he had been.

adit—an almost horizontal entrance to a mine, from the Latin *aditus*, access—so too we enter parts of the mind, illuminating the sloped walls there, where a friend of a man dead a year to the day (just as we turn our clocks) enters through a slit, like the grin of the moon, in some moment, some movement that brings not her own but his thin smile to her lips.

Bells

What if we saw our hearts as if for the first time—
one sitting like a Buddha,
another, shuffling like a man without a home.
Compassion means the heart's desire, bright or bitter, counts twice—
like a king in checkers. Like a lover's words
when he touches certain scars;
all these years later the wound's doubly fierce, doubly
healed, and the morning is a rosy glove
pulled onto your whole body.
You hear the bells from the seminary,
and for as long as they ring, your heart is without a wish.

commensurate—of equal extent or duration, from the Latin *com* +

mesuratus, measure—she recalls her own nights not breathing, the

window wide open, and gauges her difficulties no less. Her friend's

daughter, so facilely lovely in her gingham-checked dress and Nikes,

carries her atomizer everywhere in a heart-sized purse. A shame, it seems,

but there are stars everywhere, often on paths we can't see, no doubt

paired with us.

spring   coming on

a man looks down the barrel of his woe
                              and is spoken to
by a little green flame
                    he puts down the gun   and walks away
the way he walked away
from that hamburger-stand on the coast of Maine, years ago
                    when his problems were but blossoms

this is not to say he forgets about his troubles
                    but that the door is open, after weeks of cold

45

Blossom

I would be sitting in reading group, he said. *A butterfly would come in the window, and I would be gone.* The hearing in his right ear is gone. Now, he lies in bed,waiting for the anti-vertigo pill to take hold. The hearing may come back. He would always return to the book before him, eventually. And the teacher's stern look would fade. All day long, he listens to a vestibule of flies, stars fizzling in his inner ear. *The Chinese word for fish*, he says, *sounds like rich*. Each night, before he goes to sleep, he pictures his ear as a velvety blossom; he says there is nothing more receptive, more welcoming.

flit—to move about rapidly and nimbly, from the Norwegian *flytja*, to convey—lately, he's become obsessed with Edgar Cayce. Although, reading aloud in the kitchen, he stumbles through every passage. "Herefore," he says, and she quickly corrects him. She despises her impatience, him conveying love with each word. Little moths in the flour.

Days

My realtor, whom I've called at home,
tries to pull herself together. Finally:
My neighbor's baby... the fireman drove
and the policeman held the baby—
The rain's starting up again after a few days
of sun, and that's that—soon, only rain;
as Monday, only sun. Just before the water falls
into sound, that's when we promise ourselves
to really live.

Green Card, Blue Shoes

Tired of waiting table at the Yacht Club, in June, she writes a romance novel. In July, just before she leaves for Paris, she meets a Frenchman who would like to marry her and whom she would like to marry—each has fallen in love with the other's country. They spend a week in Provence together, cherries and hazelnuts being sold in the markets. *He's like a pair of shoes I once bought,* she says. *Little blue Italian sculptures that went with nothing in my wardrobe or any future wardrobe.* When Harlequin rejects her book—*not enough sex,* she is told—she doesn't despair but begins rewriting it, switching genres, replacing the love scenes with murders.

quash—to put down or set aside forcibly, from the Latin *quassare*, to shatter—as day breaks, shattering into light. Consumed by the variety of love that breaks us, she's studying Medieval art for diversion, letting images of ascension pool in her heart, but this morning her questions link in the way of crystals; while birdsongs unspool (coo-c-o-o), she asks why, because asking eases.

surprise   coming on

you say it must smell like the shop where you work
                    full dusty moon

        pleasure pools
                        thy chuckle and drawl—
about the CFC-less Danish refrigerator: "little Danish squirrels inside"

                every moment slips
        into the moment   it was going to be

            very moon, die-cut, to be filled with itself

        just as it happens

                        thee fill me

                    for Steven Tuminello

51

Change

Waking
to the same world:
light breeze, small
northern California
town, springtime—
once again pink
flowerettes pinned
to the hawthorn,
soon the explosion
of catkins on the buckeye,
sometimes it seems
getting nowhere—
with spiritual
or material life,
though one night
a cloud of dimes
circles the bed
and the next a dream
about forgiving.

Dominoes

He works for a courier service evenings and nights, picking up envelopes from people county-wide and delivering them to the city. It was not what he'd expected to do this late in life, yet one thing had led to another. Golden State Courier Service. He had not always lived in California, but it was so long ago, the truck farms and dairy farms, the four seasons, four different girls he loved equally. Oh, maybe summer, summer evenings, had had a little more of his heart, which now, at a dog's barking, jumps like a rabbit as he climbs stairs beneath a blossoming plum tree. On the top step he catches his breath, standing out among the stars, another night knocking down the next.

3.03

What do we know? The dog nosing for a ball behind the pillow may smell its shape; a deer nibbling in a green hallway may dwell in a wholly powder-pink world, no world at all, spotted fawn by her side, straw hillside—all one.

There is a rainbow underneath each car on the rain-slick, sunlit highway, and we make a fuss because something's been forgotten, and then, there, just as we turn back down the block, the scarf lost that morning. As if He is not God but a major-domo eminently wiser than the household for which he cares. Yet he never lets on through the chance meetings, wake-up calls, and lucky days.

Fine, you say, but what about the man sleeping on his one good ear who does not hear the thief enter his house? To which I say, why be so sure that light holds more light than dark?

Innocence This Alien

Giordano's new purple salamander Smoke
takes in the world of her captor, pivoting turreted eyes,
pausing on the back of his hand—there, by the gate of all worlds.

There, at the possibilities: shoulder-high amphibians,
galaxies of treasured water spiders . . .
beauty that's not always sexual (not the Earth-quail's bobbing plume).

The salamander moves on up the boy's arm, each rubbery micro-step
plants a kiss. There is this stolen moment, and in the next, the next
heartbeat. Oh! how pretty she is, Giordano.

for Giordano Brodie

Golden Hat

The insects are living their short summer lives
as castanets, tambourines. We see it coming, the thing
we know is certain. At a crosswalk, the dream—
unsteady hand holding the rim of a golden hat.

Florid clouds tipped toward the ocean,
Johnny Appleseed clouds, a friend calls down
from an upstairs window, a light coming on in her mouth
as if a match were struck.

Peter, there's a people who believe you go on
until the very last one who's heard about you is gone.

for Peter Marlis

ersatz—being a substitute, an imitation, from the German *ersetzen*, replacement—he finds a note on the formica table in his mother's script and when a friend calls can't finish a sentence, having written a check only hours ago to the crematorium and being left with a sense of her in the room, hovering over her coffee; the collie's still sitting at her feet, begging.

Hollywood

Ten million of us in this sprawling net,
this Bombay, Mexico City, this L.A.

Thursday evening a few blocks from the old
movie lots, Beautiful Ruth, unemployed and

on her third day without a cigarette; happy—
her throat finally sore, the first sign of withdrawal.

Out on her art deco veranda: after-dinner stillness,
a car sliding into the garage below.

Ten feet from Ruth's, behind a pulled shade
a man empties his pockets; you can't know much

about a man setting down keys and change
on a silhouetted dresser—he may wake up

as he did yesterday, complaining,
or as he did today, calling out *Olé, olé.*

echo—a repetition, a remnant, from the Greek *ekho:* Echo, pining away until nothing but her cry remained—his washing the windows of the rented truck makes the same sound as the desert doves on wires, at windows, everywhere since Emily's death, repeatedly descending and ascending, small and peacemaking. As she was, whose house he has packed up. One bird watching, then another.

Aquarium

Peter has grown old and sentimental—
Nothing, he says, *brings more joy to my heart*
than watching, even on television, someone being kind
to someone else.
In their tank at the San Francisco Aquarium, the herring
seem to be lighting the way for one another.
Every third or fourth fish holds open its mouth a few seconds
like a coin return on a pay phone,
and the spoon-sized head shines a bright aluminum
within the gray nebula of four-inch swimmers.
What if we made a choice
at the end of another life we've all but forgotten,
and that of all the worlds we might have chosen,
all the multiple worlds, we chose this one,
where kindness is possible?

Stardust

In a small history of the Great Plains
a band of Indians plunders a keelboat
stowing fortunes of gold dust
in buckskin sacks. Once the cargo
is theirs, they keep the durable,
the leather—for packing chokecherries
and buffalo—let the gold
mix with the sand, the element gimcrack,
stardust to the Sioux.
And pausing in my reading
I juxtapose romance
against these work-mastered days,
love's ticking metal, the sparkle-
mask of unworkable love, neither steady
nor enduring. Gleaming, luring.

Butter

Go figure. The daylilies' yellow deepens gloriously
as night settles in. Which seems the way with things earthly.

And as evening glorifies a garden, a story deepens—
flooding a listener's heart, swinging it open:

an early Polynesian
setting sail by the stars and the blue tones of the ocean;

a man with a basset hound shouting at his wedding guests;
years ago, a boy on a train, a fuchsia on his lap.

You could enter through the gate of any one of them,
recalling the tale over and over

like a tiger chasing its tail until its body turns to butter.
(Love, I want to say to you now, isn't it the way?)

You may hear a story, and it may not bring you to love just then;
it may be years later that you learn enough and soften.

for Nina Wise

Stefanie Marlis's first book of poetry, *Slow Joy*, won the Brittingham Prize from the University of Wisconsin in 1989 and the Great Lakes Colleges Association New Writers Award in 1990. She has received a fellowship from the National Endowment for the Arts, as well as three California prizes: two Marin Arts Council Awards and the Joseph Henry Jackson Award. Her work has been published in numerous journals, including *Zyzzyva*, *Arshile*, *American Poetry Review*, *Poetry*, *Manoa*, *The Gettysburg Review*, and *Volt*. Marlis has taught at the College of Marin, San Francisco State University, and the University of San Francisco. She now makes her living as a freelance copywriter. In this capacity, she has recently written a book entitled *The Art of the Bath* for Chronicle Books. Marlis lives in San Anselmo, California, with her dog, Io.

Eliot Holtzman